Starting with Words

Anne Rooney

QED Publishing

First published in the UK in 2005 by
QED Publishing
A Quarto Group company
226 City Road
London EC1V 2TT

www.qed-publishing.co.uk

A Catalogue record for this book is available from
the British Library.

ISBN 1 84538 188 2

Written by Anne Rooney
Consultant Philip Stubbs
Designed by Jacqueline Palmer
Editor Louisa Somerville
Illustrator John Haslam
Illustrations page 29 Luki Sumner-Rooney
Photographer Ray Moller
Models provided by Scallywags

Publisher Steve Evans
Creative Director Louise Morley
Editorial Manager Jean Coppendale

Anne Rooney has asserted her right under
the Copyright, Designs and Patents Act 1988
to be identified as the author of this work.

Printed and bound in China

Words in bold **like this** are explained in the Glossary on page 30.

Contents

About Starting with Words   4

Starting to type   6

Words and sentences   8

New lines   10

Arranging words   12

Word banks   14

Making changes   16

A bit different   18

Big and small   20

Get it right   22

Print your work   24

Over to you   26

Glossary   30

Index   31

Grown-up zone   32

About Starting with Words

TISSUES

SOAP FLAKES

Cornflakes

We use printed
words to tell people things.
Can you see printed words all
around you? You'll find them
on posters, books, labels,
packets, comics and even
on your clothes!

Flower Power

Ghost Stories

BAKED BEANS

You can print words on
a computer. Sometimes this is
more useful than writing with
a pen or pencil.

Ibrahim
Smith
class 1a
History

Ibrahim
Smith
class 1a
Geography

Ibrahim
Smith
class 1a
English

Ibrahim
Smith
class 1a
Art

A computer helps to make your work neater. You can make changes without your writing getting messy. You can print lots of copies, too.

You are invited to Jade's Party

Starting to type

You can use the keyboard to **type** words in a **document** on the computer.

Making letters

The keyboard has a key for each letter – and some other keys, which we'll look at later.

To make a letter appear on the screen, press the key with the letter that you want, then lift your finger off it again straight away.

If you hold down a key, the same letter will appear again – and again, and again!

lots of kisses
XXXXXXXXX

Shift
key

Capitals

To begin a sentence, or at the start of a name, you need a **capital letter**.

To make a capital letter, hold down the Shift key and then press the letter. Let go of both keys when you see the letter appear on screen.

Practise!

Type your name, starting with a capital letter.

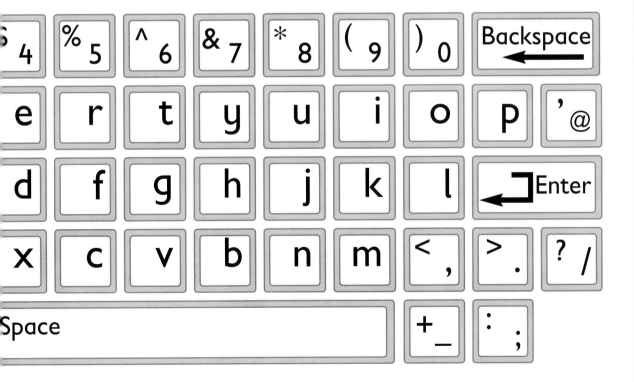

Words and sentences

To make whole sentences you need to add spaces between words and use full stops.

Space between words

At the end of a word, press the Space bar at the bottom of the keyboard. Then start the next word.

Oops!

If you make a mistake when you're typing, press the Backspace or Delete key.

This takes away the last thing you typed – just like rubbing it out!

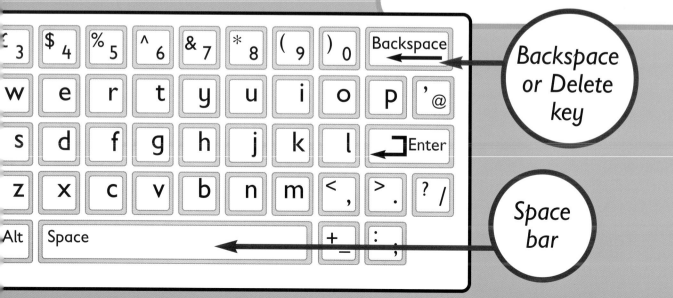

Backspace or Delete key

Space bar

Full stops

Each sentence needs a capital letter at the start and a full stop at the end.

The full stop key looks like this:

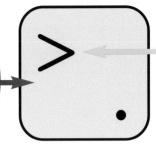

Just press the key to get a full stop.

? Can you find the key for a full stop on the keyboard?

If you hold down the Shift key while you press the full stop key, you'll get the **>** at the top.

Numbers

There's a key for each number – they're along the top of the keyboard.

Practise!

Try copying this sentence:
My dog is big and friendly.

New lines

If you want to make a longer piece of writing, such as a story, you'll need to write more than one line.

Starting a new line

If you type a whole line of words, the computer will start a new line for you on its own – you don't need to do anything.

But if you want to start a new line before you've got to the end, press the Enter key.

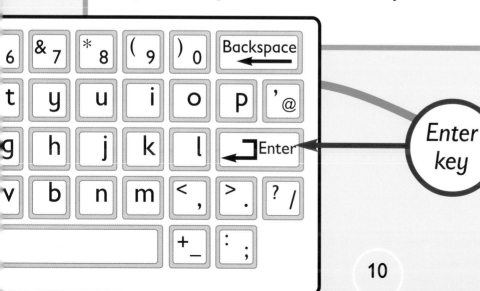

Enter key

10

You need to start new lines when you make a list, type an address or make a set of labels.

We have moved house.
My new address is:

We have moved house.
My new address is:

Lucy Brown
4 Lilac End
West Town
BL4 9ER

Practise!

Copy this list.
You can change the favourites if you like.

My favourite animals are:

1. sharks
2. earwigs
3. hamsters

For my birthday
I would like:

a new bike
a puppet
a football
some books

Arranging words

You can space your words and lines out on the page to make your work look better – or a bit special.

Writing poems

When you write a poem, you'll need to start lots of new lines.

You might also want to leave an empty line between verses.

Press Enter twice to do this.

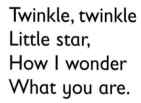

Twinkle, twinkle
Little star,
How I wonder
What you are.

Up above
The world so high,
Like a diamond
In the sky.

Twinkle, twinkle
Little star,
How I wonder
What you are.

You can use the Space bar to arrange words in your poem, too.

Humpty Dumpty sat on the wall

Humpty Dumpty had a great

F
A
L
L

Letter pictures

You can even make pictures from letters and spaces.

```
egg              H      H
eggegg           H      H
eggeggegg        HHHH
eggeggegg        H      H
eggegg           H      H
egg
```

Practise!

Can you type the word 'triangle' over and over to make a triangle?

```
          tri
         angle
       triangletri
     angletriangletri
   angletriangletriangle
 triangletriangletriangletri
```

Word banks

It can take a long time to type your words when you start using the computer. At school, your computer might have a **word bank** so that you can pick a word without having to type it.

Hello

What is a word bank?

A word bank is a list of words on the screen. Your teacher will probably have made a special bank of words you need for the work you are doing.

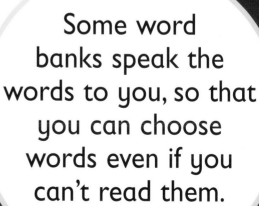

Some word banks speak the words to you, so that you can choose words even if you can't read them.

Old Mother Hubbard
gave her dog |

Click
word
then

Click to
listen

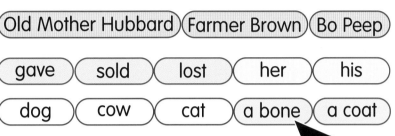

(Old Mother Hubbard) (Farmer Brown) (Bo Peep)

(gave) (sold) (lost) (her) (his)

(dog) (cow) (cat) (a bone) (a coat)

Choosing a word

You might need to click on the word, and then on a button, to listen to the word or copy it into your work. It's a good idea to listen to all the words so that you pick the best one.

For lunch today I ate ....

pizza	salad	pasta	apple
banana	cheese	chicken	tomato

click to
choose

Making changes

Sometimes you need to make changes to your work.
You might have made a mistake, or thought of a better way to do your work.

Adding words

You can add more words anywhere you want in your document.

Just click where you want to make a change and start typing. The new words will appear in between the words you've already got.

The Three Frogs

The Three Pink Spotty Frogs

click and type

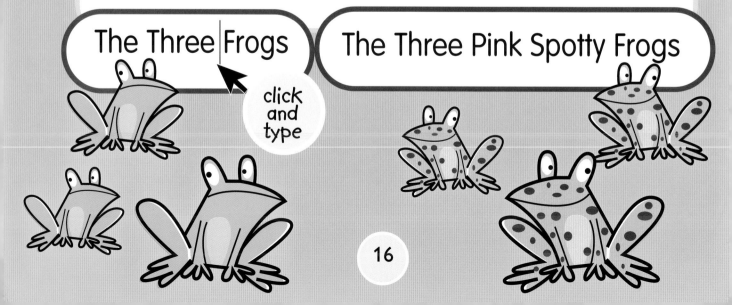

Adding space

To add a space between words, click where you want the space and then press the Space bar.

twowords

two words

click here
and press
Space bar

You can split up a line, too, or add more blank lines. Click where you want to split or add a line and press Enter.

Spelling book Carl

click here
and press
Enter

Spelling book
Carl

Practise! Type this: I like birds and fish.

and change it to this: I like blue birds and green fish.

17

A bit different

Sometimes you might want to make several documents that are slightly different. It's easy to change what you've typed – you don't need to type it all again.

Changing words

Sometimes you will want to replace one word with another.

Dear Sarah

Please come to my party on Saturday at 3pm.

Love Rachel

Sarah

click and hold

1. Put the mouse pointer at the start of the word.

Take it away

If you want to get rid of some words completely, you can do it like this.

> I don't like football.

> I like football.

1. Highlight the word, just as if you were going to change it.

2. Press the Delete or Backspace key to take the word away.

Sar|ah

Sarah|

Lily|

2. Press the mouse button and move the mouse along to **highlight** the word.

3. Take your finger off the mouse button when the word is highlighted.

4. Type in your new word.

Dear Lily

Please come to my party on Saturday at 3pm.

Love Rachel

Big and small

If you look around you, you'll see that words are printed in different sizes.

LOST CAT

Ziggy

A white cat with a tabby patch on his head.
Please call 000 7960 0759

Big and bold

If something has to be read from a long way away, or it's important that people notice it, it's usually printed in large letters.

STOP!

The words in books for young children are usually printed in large sizes with only a few words on each page. Books for adults have lots of words that are in smaller print.

cat

dog

ball

kite

Volcanoes

Volcanoes are mountains that spurt fire and hot rock into the air.

They can be very dangerous. The hot rock from a volcano comes originally from far underground. The Earth has a layer of molten hot rock 3000 kilometres thick.

In newspapers, headings are bigger than the rest of the words so that you notice them first.

Daily News • 20 July 2005

Grrreat escape!

A dangerous Bengal tiger escaped yesterday afternoon from a zoo in Hamburg.

Dinosaurs
Year 2 Class Project

Some of the biggest dinosaurs ate plants.

Some ancient reptiles could even fly. They were bigger than birds.

Your work

Your teacher will set the size of words for you when you use the computer at school.

You would use bigger letters for a poster or wall display than for a label to go on your drawer.

Joe Young

Get it right

Always check your work when you've finished. Make sure you haven't done anything wrong.

Read through your work

- Are the words spelled correctly?
- Have you left spaces between the words?
- Have you used **punctuation** and capital letters properly?
- Is there enough space between the **paragraphs**?
- If you find any mistakes, put them right.

my freind iscalled alice

My friend is called Alice.

Even better

Can you think of ways of making your work better?

a **big** cake

Try a more interesting word – a 'huge' cake instead of a 'big' cake, or a boy who 'jumped' out of bed instead of 'got' out of bed.

a **huge** cake

Make any changes and then check your work again.

Toby **got** out of bed.

Toby **jumped** out of bed.

Get help

Ask someone else to look at your work. They might spot a mistake you have missed. Or they might think of a way of making it better.

Print your work

It's nice to do your work on the computer – but even better if you can print it out to show to other people or take home!

Getting ready to print

Before you print your work, check it carefully so that you don't waste paper printing it with lots of mistakes.

What colour?

You might be able to print your work on coloured paper. It's a good way to make it stand out.

Come to our Christmas play on Friday

Printing

There is a print button on the screen. Click on it to print your work on paper.

Another look

Read through your work after you have printed it. If you spot any more mistakes, put them right and print it out again!

Over to you

On the next four pages, find out how to type and print your own story!

Think of a story…

Think of a story you'd like to write. It can be a story you've made up, or a fairy story or another story you've heard or read.

Draw pictures for the story on four sheets of paper.

?

Are there people talking? If so, you could draw empty **speech bubbles** on your pictures.

Type the words

Now type out the words for your story on the computer.

Leave a blank line after each sentence.

Jess found an egg on the ground.

She made a nest and a bird to look after it.

She kept the egg warm.

She waited for it to hatch.

The egg started to crack.

Now type the words for the speech bubbles.

Do not write too much or your words will not fit into the bubbles you have drawn.

Come on, you can do it.

Snap

Cut and stick

Check your work, make any changes, and then print it out.

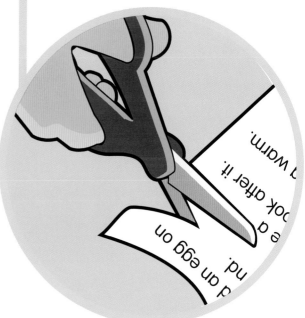

Cut up the page so that each sentence is on a separate strip.

Stick the words in the right places on your story pages.

Now print out the speech words. Cut the words up and stick them inside the speech bubbles in the right places.

Jess found an egg on the ground.

1

She made a nest and a bird to look after it.

She kept the egg warm. 2

She waited for it to hatch.

Come on, you can do it.

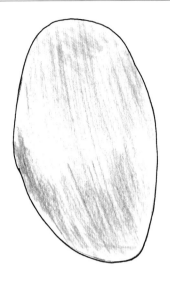

The egg started to crack. 3

Hurrah!

Snap

It was a baby crocodile! 4

Glossary

Capital letter   Big letter, such as A, B or C (instead of a, b or c).

Document   Piece of typed work on the computer.

Highlight   Show up brightly; on the computer, highlighted words appear on a coloured background.

Paragraph   Block of writing made up of one or more sentences.

Punctuation   Full stop, comma, dash or other mark that helps us to read a sentence.

Speech bubble   In a picture, a line drawn around the words a person is saying.

Type   To press keys on the keyboard to make writing appear on the screen.

Word bank   Set of words to choose from to use in your work.

Index

Backspace key 8, 19

big letters 20–21

blank lines 12, 17, 27

capital letters 7, 9, 30

changes 5, 16–17

checking work 22–23, 24, 25, 28

colour 24

computers 4–5

Delete key 8, 19

document 6, 16, 18, 30

Enter key 10, 12, 27

full stops 8, 9

highlight 19, 30

keyboard 6–7, 8, 9, 10

letter pictures 13

letters 6–7

lines:
blank 12, 17, 27
new 10–11, 12
splitting 17

making changes 5, 16–17, 18, 23

mistakes 8, 16, 22, 23, 25

mouse pointer 18–19

newspaper headings 21

new lines 10

numbers 9

pages 27, 28, 29

paragraph 22, 30

poems 12

print size 20–1

printing 4–5, 24–25

punctuation 22, 30

screen 6

sentences 7, 8, 9, 27, 28

Shift key 6, 7, 9

Space bar 8, 13, 17, 27

spaces 8, 12, 17

speech bubbles 26, 27, 28, 29, 30

splitting lines 17

story 26–29

type 6–7, 30

word bank 14–15, 30

words 8
adding 16
arranging 12–13
changing 18–19
removing 19
replacing 18–19

Grown-up zone

Starting with Words
and the National Curriculum

This book will help a child to cover work unit 1b, part of unit 1c and unit 2a of the IT Scheme of Work for the National Curriculum for England and Wales.

It can be tied in with work in the literacy framework, or be used to help children to present project work for history, geography or science. This can be achieved by tasks such as encouraging

your children to collect and discuss all kinds of printed information. Help your children to identify the purpose and intended audience of the materials they find and to discuss the message they think the information is trying to communicate. Ask whether the presentation is suitable, and if the message gets across.

Encourage your children to review, evaluate and improve their own work at all stages. If possible, show them work by older children and help them to see how this fulfils the same aims that they have in their own work.